OFFICE OF SCIENTIFIC INTELLIGENCE: THE ORIGINAL WIZARDS OF ★ LANGLEY

A Symposium Commemorating 60 Years of S&T Intelligence Analysis

TABLE OF CONTENTS

I. Overview of the Office of Scientific Intelligence **4**

II. OSI Timeline **12-13**

III. The Birth of OSI
  General Order Number 13 .... **14**
  Background section from Weber history **16**
  Sherman Kent memo on S&T intelligence **24**

IV. Intelligence Products
  Soviet Bloc Capabilities though 1957 .... **29**
  [NIE-65]

  The Sovirt Atomic Energy Program to Mid-1957 .. **34**
  [NIE 11-3A-54]

  Soviet Capabilities and Probable Programs
  in the Guided Missle Feild **39**
  [NIE 11-6-54]

  Soviet Guided Missle Capabilities
  and Probable Programs **44**
  [NIE 11-12-55]

The Historical Collections Division (HCD) of the Office of Information Management Services is responsible for executing the CIA's Historical Review Program. This program seeks to identify, collect, and review for possible release to the public significant historical information. The mission of HCD is to:

- Provide an accurate, objective understanding of the information and intelligence that has helped shape the foundation of major US policy decisions.

- Improve access to lessons learned, presenting historical material to emphasize the scope and context of past actions.

- Improve current decision-making and analysis by facilitating reflection on the impacts and effects arising from past decisions.

- Uphold Agency leadership commitments to openness, while protecting the national security interests of the US.

- Provide the American public with valuable insight into the workings of their Government.

CENTER FOR THE STUDY OF INTELLIGENCE

The History Staff in the CIA Center for the Study of Intelligence fosters understanding of the Agency's history and its relationship to today's intelligence challenges by communicating instructive historical insights to the CIA workforce, other US Government agencies, and the public. CIA historians research topics on all aspects of Agency activities and disseminate their knowledge through publications, courses, briefings, and Web-based products. They also work with other Intelligence Community historians on publication and education projects that highlight interagency approaches to intelligence issues. Lastly, the CIA History Staff conducts an ambitious program of oral history interviews that are invaluable for preserving institutional memories that are not captured in the documentary record.

The Weapons Intelligence, Nonproliferation, and Arms Control Center (WINPAC) is the Directorate of Intelligence's focal point for analysis and policy support on foreign weapons and technology, nonproliferation, and arms control-related issues. WINPAC's areas of responsibility include:

- The production of all-source intelligence relating to the threat of foreign strategic weapons, to include nuclear, biological and chemical weapons (WMD); missile and space systems; and emerging conventional threats and countermeasures.

- Monitoring compliance to arms control, nonproliferation, and threat reduction regimes; support to treaty negotiation and implementation; strategic interdiction of WMD-related networks.

- Collection programs and specialized signals intelligence analyses.

WINPAC and—to a lesser extent—the Office of Transnational Issues now embrace much of what was in the Office of Scientific Intelligence when it and the Office of Weapons Intelligence were merged in 1980.

The Directorate of Science and Technology (DS&T) is the Central Intelligence Agency's lead component for tackling technical challenges. The Directorate history can be traced back to the years 1954 through 1962 when the U-2 program was conceived and the Director of Central Intelligence (DCI) consolidated the scientific and technical talents of the CIA. DS&T offices create and apply innovative technology to meet intelligence needs. The Directorate's work ranges from exploratory research to the design, development, and operation of specialized intelligence systems, both large and small. The Directorate is actively engaged in every collection discipline: imagery intelligence (IMINT), signals intelligence (SIGINT), human sources intelligence (HUMINT), and measurement and signature intelligence (MASINT). By providing critical technology and technical know-how, it also supports all phases of the intelligence process, from collection through analysis and dissemination of the intelligence product.

OVERVIEW OF THE OFFICE OF ★SCIENTIFIC INTELLIGENCE

THE OFFICE OF SCIENTIFIC INTELLIGENCE: WAGING AND WINNING THE COLD WAR

This overview and collection of documents and other material related to the Office of Scientific Intelligence (OSI) offer a glimpse of CIA's overall contribution to the analysis of Soviet capabilities in science and technology during the Cold War. It is by no means intended to be definitive, or even complete, with respect to all the activities associated with the Agency's scientific and technological capabilities, analysis, and resulting reporting. It does, however, highlight some key events and selected activities that contribute to our understanding of the unique role OSI played in the Agency's history.[1]

---

[1] This overview is excerpted in large part from Clarence E. Smith's essay on CIA's Analysis of Soviet Science and Technology in Watching the Bear: Essays on CIA's Analysis of the Soviet Union, published in 1996. "Smitty" was a long-time career analyst and manager in the Defensive Systems Division of the Office of Scientific Intelligence, who later served as a senior manager in the Intelligence Community Staff as the Vice Chairman of the Committee on Imagery Requirements and Exploitation and as a Special Assistant to the Director of Central Intelligence.

The period following World War II saw unparalleled growth in technological developments, and nowhere was this truer than in the East-West competition during the Cold War. New and technological capabilities on both sides offered opportunities for new weapons and new collection techniques. The prospect of new Soviet capabilities led US policymakers to demand that we understand not only the new technologies (for our own purposes) but also the extent and nature of Soviet capabilities. Urgent new collection requirements necessitated new, more sophisticated means of collection, which in turn required new technical analysis techniques and capabilities. The data acquired by these new collection systems often helped clarify gaps in our intelligence. Thus, the need for scientific and technical intelligence on the Soviet Union generated a whole new set of requirements for new sources and methods, many of which remain current today.

With this as background, it is clear that the development of technical intelligence capabilities at CIA[2] led to significant successes in the analysis of Soviet S&T capabilities. A corollary to this development was that it led to major bureaucratic and organizational changes within CIA and the wider Intelligence Community. The major expansion of CIA's technical intelligence capabilities provided unique advantages to the United States and its allies in waging and winning the Cold War.

THE NEED FOR S&T INTELLIGENCE

The emergence of the Cold War accelerated the development of ever more technically advanced weapons and generated early recognition of the need for additional technical intelligence. For US policymakers this meant obtaining data on Soviet weapons developments and operational concepts, identifying important new systems and, most important, developing the technical means for collecting and processing such data.

US intelligence on Soviet nuclear weapons development played an especially important role in the initial extension of technical intelligence into the Cold War. In this regard, the transfer of the Manhattan Project intelligence group from the Department of State to the new

---

2 Technical intelligence (including collection, processing, and analysis)—as a new, distinct discipline—was not unique to CIA. It was integral to the Intelligence Community as a whole, as well as to the military services, nonintelligence elements of the Department of Defense, other federal government agencies, and related private-sector entities.

CIA enabled the Agency to build its scientific and technical intelligence capabilities. The complexity of the technical structure of the Soviet nuclear weapons development program and the many distinctive observables associated with it provided a classic technical intelligence challenge to US analysts. In particular, the Soviet program demanded technical data that could be obtained only by new collection techniques.

By the 1950s, it was clear that the USSR possessed both nuclear weapons and the means of long-range delivery. But key questions remained for US policymakers. How far advanced and how effective were these capabilities? Could they be used against the continental United States as well as its allies? The answers to these questions were fundamental to US strategic deterrence.

Technical intelligence was the primary tool US officials used to address these questions. Because the USSR, Eastern Europe, and China were "denied areas," they posed difficult challenges to traditional forms of human and military reconnaissance collection. These countries were highly efficient police states that severely restricted internal movement and contacts with foreigners; they also had effective, modern air defenses. This meant traditional means of espionage and reconnaissance were limited in providing the needed information, much less access, by the West to Soviet Bloc weapons designers and remote test sites.

To counter this, CIA and the Intelligence Community developed new and innovative collection approaches, including overhead systems to collect images. These new systems allowed US analysts to discover the physical characteristics and locations of weapons, test ranges, operational sites, and support structures. Signals intelligence (SIGINT) collectors in these new systems eavesdropped on military exercises and administrative communications. Telemetry collectors intercepted and recorded the instrumentation signals transmitted by weapons undergoing tests; blast-detection sensors assessed the power of a detonation. Signal and power collectors measured emitter specifications, and there were a host of other collection techniques. S&T collection assets were deployed, both in the air and in space, under sea, and on the periphery of the USSR and were placed clandestinely within the USSR itself.

The lack of hard intelligence facts and having few human intelligence resources within the Soviet Bloc were the key drivers in developing both US aircraft and satellite imaging and signals intelligence collection systems. In addition to the actual technical collection, however, there was a parallel development in the analytical field as US analysts sought to make sense of the raw data. The challenge to the Intelligence Community was not only to create new collection methods but also to be able to derive useful information from the resultant data. The CIA's Office of Scientific Intelligence, and later the Directorate of Science and Technology (DS&T), was in the forefront of the development of both the new technical intelligence collection systems and the expanded analytical capabilities.

The intelligence reports and estimates included in this collection cover the period from the early 1950s through the mid- to late 1960s, and the effect of advancements in technical collection and analysis is readily apparent. There were no disagreements within the Intelligence Community on Soviet capabilities as surveyed in National Intelligence Estimate (NIE) 11-5-59, *Soviet Capabilities in Guided Missiles and Space Vehicles*, but by October 1964 (in NIE 11-8-64) debates had emerged over both the capabilities and the number of deployed sites for Soviet intercontinental ballistic missiles (ICBMs). These disagreements primarily resulted from having more data which meant more opportunities to have different interpretations of the available information. Similarly, in the defensive missile area, Intelligence Community analysts using the same data now disagreed in NIE 11-3-65 over whether and how the Soviets were upgrading their surface-to-air missiles (SAMs). These strategic offensive and defensive missile concerns stayed in the forefront of the intelligence debate well into the 1970s.

SCIENTIFIC AND TECHNICAL INTELLIGENCE ISSUES

In the course of the Cold War, any number of issues arose that had to be addressed urgently by means of technical intelligence. In time, OSI and the Intelligence Community at large acquired an infrastructure of techniques, tools, facilities, and technical specialists that was able to respond to new questions as they arose. Some of the key issues are not surprising:

- Soviet nuclear weapons developments dominated in the early years, shifting later to matters of weapons and material inventories, compliance with testing agreements, and the transfer of nuclear technology to potential proliferators.

- Soviet ballistic missile development and deployment stayed high on the priority list throughout, but also underwent many changes of focus--counting numbers, determining characteristics, and monitoring for compliance with arms control agreements.

- The Soviet space challenge began with a burst of publicity and quickly became a matter of US military concern but did not materialize as a real threat issue.

- Soviet air defenses, antiballistic missile (ABM), and SAM missile upgrades became entangled with one another throughout the period, producing great concern and posing one of the most severe challenges to US technical intelligence.

- Chemical and biological warfare concerns emerged (and continue to this day), plagued by uncertainties and posing extraordinarily difficult intelligence problems, primarily because of the type of collection access required.

- Arms-control monitoring emerged as a highly defined issue and intelligence problem with the early nuclear weapons testing agreements and leapt to the forefront with the negotiation and conclusion of agreements with the Soviets covering reduction of arms and forces and qualitative constraints.

Two other issues that generated attention were (1) the assessments of existing and emerging Soviet scientific and technical capabilities (such as stealth and supercomputers), and (2) the detailed characterization of the Soviet research and development cycle that led to the fielding of advanced (and sometimes unexpected) Soviet weaponry, achievements in space, or scientific breakthroughs.

THE BIRTH OF OSI

As early as 1946, when the Cewntral Intelligence Group (CIG) was established, the need for scientific intelligence was recognized. Its importance was further emphasized in the 1948 report of the Eberstadt Task Force of the Hoover Commission, which stressed the likely overriding importance of scientific and technical intelligence and the need for a central authority responsible for assimilating all scientific information from abroad as well as competent to estimate its significance. The report concluded that "failure to properly appraise the extent of scientific developments in enemy countries may have more immediate and catastrophic consequences than failure in any other field of intelligence."[3] Recognizing the importance of scientific and technical intelligence, CIA on 31 December 1948 created the Office of Scientific Intelligence (OSI), an organization that brought together the collectors and the processors of intelligence information.

Concern that other countries might develop nuclear weapons and an awareness that advanced knowledge was the only practical shield against a surprise attack fed a sense of urgency among US policymakers. Concern extended to biological and chemical warfare and to the likely development of guided missiles, which would increase the danger of surprise attack on the continental United States. Despite such concern, little real progress took place until President Harry Truman's 23 September 1949 announcement of the first Soviet nuclear explosion. The next month the Director of Central Intelligence (DCI) created the Scientific Intelligence Committee (SIC) to coordinate the entire US scientific intelligence effort.

The required coordination, however, did not come easily. CIA chaired this new committee, charged with responsibility for scientific and technical intelligence, including all research and development up to the initiation of weapons systems series production. This concept was opposed by the US military, which sought to distinguish between basic scientific capabilities and weapons systems applications and keep the latter to itself.

There was some support for CIA's having this responsibility even within the defense establishment itself, however. The Research and Development Board in the Department of Defense, for example, was extremely dissatisfied with the intelligence support it received from the military intelligence agencies and supported the SIC as its primary source of intelligence support. Because of OSI's competence in Soviet nuclear capabilities, the military also accepted the Joint Atomic Energy Intelligence Committee (JAEIC) as a subcommittee of SIC, to be concerned with that subject exclusively. Shortly thereafter, other subcommittees were established on biological warfare, chemical warfare, electronics and guided missiles, and later on aircraft and antiaircraft weapons systems.[4]

The services did not give up, however. During the early 1950s, there was a long struggle within the SIC between its military and civilian members: Army-Navy-Air Force versus CIA-State-Atomic Energy Commission. In August 1952, the original directive establishing SIC (OSI's lifeline) was rescinded. A new directive dissolved the SIC and all of its subcommittees except the JAEIC. It was retained as a subcommittee of the interdepartmental Intelligence Advisory Committee itself. The intelligence agencies of the Department of Defense were given primary intelligence production responsibility with regard to weapons, weapon systems, and military equipment and techniques, including intelligence on related scientific research and development. The new directive assigned to CIA's OSI primary responsibility for scientific research in general, fundamental research in the basic sciences, and medicine (other than military medicine). The Defense Department agencies as well as CIA were now given responsibility for atomic energy intelligence, the original basis for CIA's scientific and technical effort.

The new directive had a negative impact on the morale of OSI. In reaction, it began to devote less attention and energy to asserting CIA's authority to coordinate scientific intelligence and more to developing its own capabilities for research in all fields of scientific intelligence, including weapon systems development in anticipation of a day when a new DCI would value such independent capabilities.

---

3 Department of State, *Foreign Relations of the United States: Emergence of the Intelligence Establishment*, 1945-1950 (Washington, DC: US Government Printing Office, 1996), p. 1012.

4 Several noted scientists in the Boston area, involved in US weapons-system developments and very concerned about the lack of US intelligence on corresponding Soviet developments, approached CIA/OSI in late 1950 and offered to assist. This group included the men who became the first three Presidential Scientific Advisors: James Killian, George Kistiakowski, and Jerome Weisner. They constituted what was known as the Boston Scientific Advisory Panel and were very valuable to OSI.

While OSI refocused its efforts in the Directorate of Intelligence (DI), there was a similar growth in electronic intelligence (ELINT) collection capabilities within CIA's Directorate of Plans, later to be known as the Directorate of Operations (DO). CIA's ELINT efforts furthered its scientific and technical credentials through the 1950s. With the advent of the U-2 and later technical collection programs, it continued to grow. By the time S&T activity was first consolidated at CIA—in a Directorate of Research in 1962—there were well-established organizational units dedicated to scientific and technical intelligence in both the Directorate of Plans and OSI.

CREATING A NEW DIRECTORATE

It was the creation of CIA's DS&T by DCI John McCone in 1963, however, that finally brought together the key scientific and technical functions from the DI, the DO, and the short-lived research directorate. From that point, true synergy began with respect to scientific and technical collection and analysis at CIA. And it did so—with Albert (Bud) Wheelon as the Agency's first Deputy Director for Science and Technology (DDS&T)—at a moment in history when decisive action was required.

A tremendous breadth of technical disciplines was drawn together in the new directorate. The DI's OSI, concerned with basic scientific research conducted by foreign countries, became a part, as did a computer services group from the DI. The Office of ELINT (OEL), which had some of it origins in OSI, came from the Directorate of Plans. The Development Projects Division, which had been responsible for developing the U-2, the A-12 OXCART, and the CORONA overhead systems, now joined the new directorate as did the Office of Research and Development, charged with applying new technologies to intelligence, and the Foreign Missile and Space Analysis Center (FMSAC), a group established to monitor foreign missile and space programs.

Wheelon did not merely create a new organization, however. The usefulness of the U-2 airborne reconnaissance program against the Soviet Union had ended in 1960 with the shootdown of Gary Powers, and new ways to gather intelligence over denied areas were needed. New intelligence technologies would have to meet the urgent requirement for reliable and comprehensive intelligence collection. The new DS&T was focused on tackling this challenge, and Wheelon became one of the earliest proponents of CIA's participation in making greater use of outer space as a venue for future intelligence collection. Wheelon greatly enhanced CIA's S&T capabilities with the integration of systems development, collection operations, data processing, and intelligence analysis.

Throughout the rest of the Cold War there were bureaucratic adjustments in the S&T directorate reflecting changing capabilities and requirements in order to integrate intelligence analysis better across multiple disciplines. OSI had spun off OEL in July 1962 and the FMSAC in November 1963. In November 1976 OSI and the Office of Weapons Intelligence (OWI)—which had been formed from FMSAC and the Defensive Systems Division of OSI in September 1973—were transferred back to the DI from DS&T in order to have all finished intelligence production under one Directorate, reversing Bud Wheelon's achievement in 1963 to secure all of CIA's S&T intelligence functions in one Directorate. At the same time, the Foreign Broadcast Information Service (FBIS) and the National Photographic Interpretations Center (NPIC) were moved to the DS&T.

The Office of Scientific Intelligence ceased to exist as an entity—after 31 years of service—when it and OWI were merged on 25 February 1980 to form the Office of Scientific and Weapons Research (OSWR), which evolved into the current Weapons Intelligence Non-Proliferation and Arms Control Center (WINPAC).

COLLECTING, PROCESSING, AND ANALYZING THE NEW DATA

The overriding problem in the early years of technical intelligence was simply gaining access to information about Soviet facilities and activities. Because of the closed Soviet society and the extensive controls on movement and access, clandestine operations launched from outside the Soviet Union had a long history of being foiled.

Nuclear issues dominated US concerns from the time of the Soviets' first atomic weapons test in 1949, but during the 1950s, new and somewhat different problems began to compete for US intelligence attention. These included Soviet bacteriological warfare and chemical warfare developments and Soviet aircraft and electronics innovations.

In the early years, before hard intelligence on Soviet developments became available, US reports on a number of Soviet scientific and technical subjects were simply derivative. For example, the basic data in a 12 October 1949 memorandum on Soviet capabilities in air-to-air guided missiles and related proximity fuses were only extrapolations of information on missiles that were under development by the Germans. Once in operation, however, US technical intelligence could exploit technical data generated during the course of Soviet weapons development or manufacture. Such data appear in many portions of the electromagnetic spectrum (visual, radio and radar signals, infrared emanations, etc.), acoustic phenomena, nuclear radioactivity, forensic samples, and material and actual equipment available for analysis. Each required a different kind of access ranging from actual physical presence in a laboratory or plant to detection from many thousands of miles distant from a specific target.

On the one hand, the United States would collect whatever it could with the access available so long as there was some hope that the collected data would shed light on the matter of concern. On the other hand, the nature of the data required would dictate the kind of access. The US focus was on Soviet air, space, naval, and defensive systems (although selected ground forces systems were sometimes assessed) and on sensors, nuclear weapons, and chemical/biological weapons. In time, it became apparent that to acquire all the key performance characteristics of any of these systems, we would need a suite of new intelligence collectors and analytic tools.

Technical intelligence was the primary tool used to address these questions. The Intelligence Community was obliged to invent new and innovative approaches to collection via remote sensors, the most well-known of which were the U-2 and OXCART manned aircraft, ELINT (i.e., radar and FIS) operations, satellite imaging, and SIGINT systems. These systems revolutionized intelligence collection.

Following the unique manned aircraft reconnaissance programs, satellite imagery provided the foundation whereby compliance with highly complex arms control provisions could be adjudged by even the most paranoid elements of national security establishments. It was quite an accomplishment.

Other collection operations were mounted on the periphery of the Soviet Union. The Berlin tunnel is an early, somewhat bizarre example of a SIGINT collection operation. More important in the long run were facilities established close to Soviet borders so as to collect signals generated at installations (targeted by means of overhead imagery) within the USSR. Electronic collection aircraft flew and ships sailed along the periphery for this same purpose.

The CORONA program, the first space-based reconnaissance program, provided an intelligence windfall for several years before the Soviets took defensive measures against it. The *Glomar Explorer*, a ship built specifically to raise a sunken Soviet submarine from the bottom of the Pacific to salvage communications equipment and nuclear components, was a feat beyond the imagination of the Soviets until the story was disclosed in the US press. These are but two examples of a highly successful technical collection program.

A significant and critical counterpart of technical collection was the ability to apply new analytical techniques to emerging collection capabilities such as telemetry and precision parametric measurements analysis from ELINT, as well as systems and processes to deal with film and then digital satellite imagery. When Soviet designers flew aircraft or missiles, they placed sensors on critical components and radioed their status to the ground so that analysis could identify problems in the event of a flight failure. While the Soviet designer had the key to which sensors were being monitored by the hundreds of telemetry traces, US intelligence analyst had to unscramble them and make sense of the reading. The challenge to the US technical community was to deliver identifiable, useable data.

The wide distribution of collection system elements and the huge amounts of data collected required a system with the capacity to pass vast amounts of data, and containing data links able to ensure the security of the information carried, able to maintain connection with a range of collection platforms and data processing facilities, and able to serve a number of data recipients. The development of these links enabled the control of collection operations as well as the retrieval of the information collected. Getting the diverse sorts of data into a form suitable for interpretation and analysis depended on major advancements in computer technology. As collection systems became more capable, the need for speed and automated handling of overwhelming quantities of information also became critical. Meeting this major technological challenge led over time to the ability of US analysts to support near-real-time delivery of data and reporting.

Not all collection systems were developed and managed by CIA. Other parts of the Intelligence Community operated aircraft, satellites, maritime resources, ground-collection sites, data links, and processing facilities. All of them tended to operate with some independence but did a remarkable job of delivering vast amounts of needed data in processed form to the many different US intelligence analysis and production organizations.

ANALYTIC ISSUES AND CAPABILITIES

By the late 1950s, the number and scope of major technical intelligence challenges facing the Agency had grown immensely. Concerns emerged about Soviet technological advances, the testing of Soviet thermonuclear weapons and, increasingly, Soviet ballistic and defensive missile developments and the Soviet space challenge. A primary response by OSI was to establish close relationships with contractors deeply involved in similar US programs, such as the Livermore and Sandia National Laboratories and various private corporations, notably TRW Incorporated. Each relationship entailed unique arrangements that allowed unusually broad access to intelligence information, wide contractor latitude in the definition of studies performed, and the inclusion of a broad tutorial role for the contractors in enhancing the capabilities of OSI analysts. These connections played a large role in developing unique technical intelligence capabilities within OSI itself.

OSI analysts of weapons systems, in addition to seeking help from the academic disciplines of science and engineering, had several core capabilities that set them apart. They were subject-matter experts, thoroughly familiar with programs of the type they were to assess, such as radar, aircraft, ICBMs, or nuclear weapons. They maintained close ties to US industry and its research and development activities. Thus, when looking at new or unfamiliar Soviet programs, they could draw on overall US experience or on relevant Soviet experience and bring insights from US development processes for similar weapons capabilities.

In addition, technical analysts were adept at team-research management. Just as it took many collectors to provide data on a specific Soviet system's characteristics, it took many technical specialists to compile all of the characteristics for a single weapon system. In the case of the Moscow Anti-Ballistic Missile system, for example, dozens of analysts were involved in assessing acquisition and engagement radars, interceptor vehicles, nuclear warheads, launchers, and command and control systems. Analysts had to be innovative and given to "out of the box" thinking as they confronted complex programs being developed by an adversary striving for technological surprises and also trying to not only minimize the information available to analysts but to mislead them if possible.

The analytical issues addressed by the S&T encompassed the discovery and assessment of hundreds of weapons and technology programs during the course of the Cold War. Many were controversial within the Intelligence Community, as four decades of declassified NIEs illustrate. Here are some examples that give a sense of the variety of the topics and challenges Soviet developments provided OSI and other IC analysts:

SS-8: Determining whether it was a new large missile or one smaller than the SS-6.

SS-9 MIRV: Determining whether the multiple warheads on the SS-9 could be independently targeted, as well as the implications of a first strike against the US missile deterrent.

SS-18 throw-weight: Assessing to what extent the large throw-weight would allow payload fractionation (additional Multiple Independently Targetable Reentry Vehicles MIRVs) without reducing the counter-silo capabilities of a single MIRV.

SS-NX-22: Determining the target-discrimination capability, reaction time and effectiveness of an advanced antiship missile intended for use against US surface combatants.

Nuclear yields: Assessing the results of weapons tests and correlating the size and yield of the device with a strategic delivery system.

SA-5 high-altitude capabilities: Determining whether unusual tests of the SA-5 portended an ABM capability.

Range of the Backfire bomber: Determining the extent to which the Backfire presented a threat against the continental US.

Alpha-class submarine: Assessing the capabilities of the world's fastest and deepest diving new submarine.

ASW detection technology: Determining the extent to which shipborn acoustic sensors or bottom-laid arrays and their associated signal-processing capabilities would permit the location or tracking of US submarines.

Soviet reconnaissance satellites: Determining the resolution capabilities of imaging satellite systems.

BMEWS battle management capabilities: Analyzing whether the ballistic missile early warning radars being built on the periphery of the USSR possessed additional, sophisticated capabilities that might facilitate the accelerated deployment of a future ABM system.

Analysts in the S&T were predominately focused on the qualitative aspects of Soviet strategic systems. Using an array of data from diverse technical collectors, human sources, and occasionally open sources, they would derive the capabilities of weapons and model them on computers. In modeling flight vehicles, for example, new data would be incorporated—the telemetry from a flight test or new external characteristics from photography—and the models refined until they conformed as closely to observed test results as possible. It became possible, for example, to run simulations of Soviet weapon system performance using data inputs collected from the Soviet's weapons systems themselves. Eventually, high confidence statements about a system's performance and limitations could be derived for use by US policymakers.

SUMMARY AND CONCLUSIONS

The development of the S&T intelligence efforts in OSI and later the DS&T and the DI produced a remarkable change in collection and analysis procedures. CIA gradually developed the organization, capabilities, and talent to identify the intelligence questions that had to be answered, to establish the data essential to answering these questions, to define ways to capture the data, and to process the data so that analysts could have hard facts in helping them resolve the problem at hand. Developing these capabilities constituted CIA's greatest contribution to US understanding of Soviet technical capabilities.

Without diminishing the contributions of the National Security Agency, the military services or the national laboratories, two developments that can be credited primarily to CIA's OSI and DS&T were of seminal importance to the assessment of the Soviet strategic threat. The first is the creation of both airborne imagery collectors and space-based imaging satellites. The second is the art of signals analysis (specifically radar systems emissions and FIS). Both were critical to addressing policymaker questions of how many, how capable, and where located. Ultimately, they made arms control agreements feasible.

First, the U-2 photography, then satellite imagery provided sufficient breadth of coverage to locate and count Soviet strike forces with relatively high confidence. Data from imaging satellites provided the basic order-of-battle inputs for the calculus of deterrence, the fundamental military strategy used by the United States during the Cold War. As film-return satellite systems were phased out and near-real-time systems introduced, the United States became increasingly confident of its ability to discern major Soviet military buildups and to give warning to policymakers and US commands. The ability of the United States to minimize the likelihood of the Soviets inflicting a "Pearl Harbor" brought with it an era of international stability despite the large numbers of nuclear weapons possessed by both sides. Thus, major strategic rivals armed with vast nuclear capabilities were able to coexist--in conflict without combat--during half a century of political and economic competition.

Telemetry and performance-measurement analysis is an arcane art form, and nowhere was it practiced more imaginatively than in OSI. It was the most productive of the sources needed to assess the qualitative capabilities of aerospace vehicles. The Soviets never understood the extent to which OSI excelled at this. As a result, from performance data collected on a wide array of flight systems came the analysis of range, fuel utilization, maneuverability, throw weight, MIRV potential, and other answers to the question of "how capable." The results were used to design US countermeasures, to calculate deterrence in qualitative and not just numerical terms, and to construct the qualitative constraints of arms limitation proposals.

In general, it can be said that OSI's contributions in producing intelligence on Soviet technical capabilities and programs came not just in the form of reports on those topics but, more important, in providing leadership in building and operating the range of capabilities that enabled such reporting. Most of the critical questions regarding Soviet systems were answered. CIA contributions were successful enough to enable the negotiation of strategic arms limitations relying heavily on the US Intelligence Community to monitor compliance with their provisions. The trust of the national security elements of the US government in the ability of the Intelligence Community to do this job is a testament to the value of the contribution it made.

CIA/OSI deserves much credit, not only for what it learned about what the Soviets were doing but, perhaps more important, for putting in place a key national asset of integrated scientific and technical intelligence collection and analysis. This is not to imply that CIA's success was achieved in isolation. It could not have been done without the support and cooperation of the military services, other government agencies, and industry. CIA's early partnership with the US Air Force was especially important in this regard and set a precedent for later cooperation.

FOOTNOTES:

[1] The term S&T is used when referring to scientific and technical intelligence, or capabilities associated with its collection or analysis, whether CIA's or elsewhere in the US Intelligence Community. S&T, even at CIA, was accomplished in many organizational elements, not only within what we know as the Directorate of Science and Technology. Many of the CIA's reports on Soviet S&T capabilities remain classified because sensitive collection methods and analytical techniques could damage current national security interests. Thus, more than with political, military, and economic intelligence issues, CIA's scientific and technical analysis available for scrutiny is included primarily in broader National Intelligence Estimates. Nevertheless, there is sufficient information available to support the conclusions of this overview. That said, this paper draws more on inference and personal insight than is the case in other disciplines.

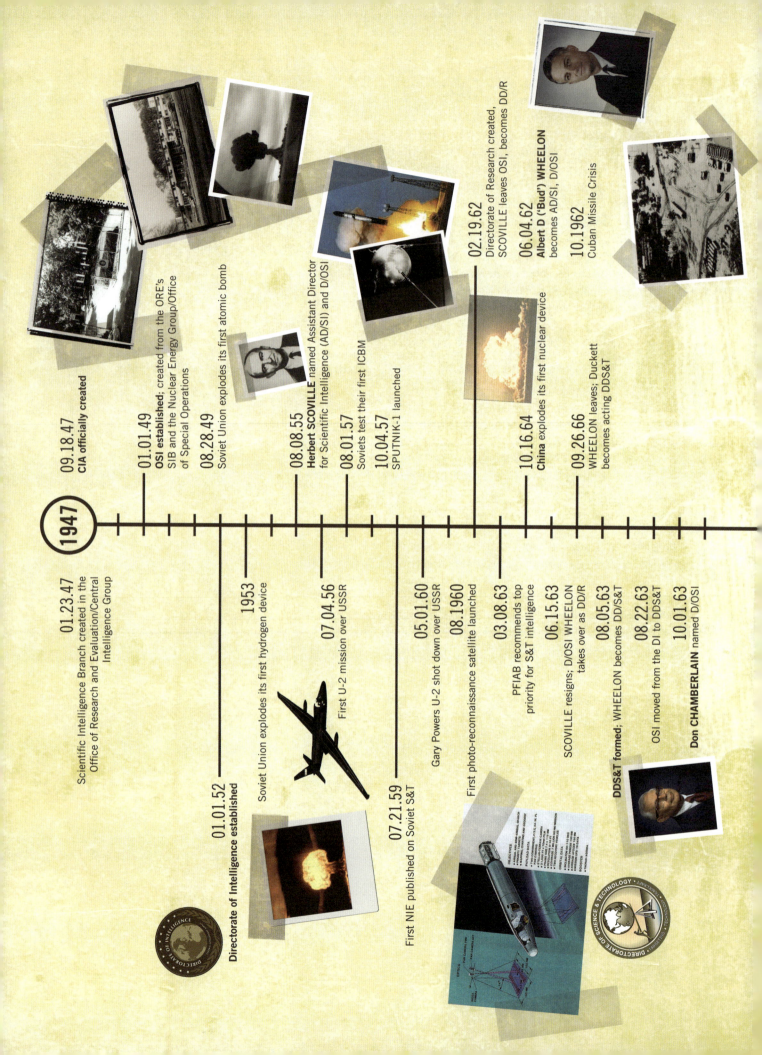

OSI TIMELINE

11.07.63 — Carl **DUCKETT** becomes Deputy Asst Director of OSI for Collection and C/GMAIC

11.07.63 — FMSAC established in DDS&T; Duckett named Chief, FMSAC

06.01.76 — Carl Duckett takes medical retirement; Les **DIRKS** becomes DDS&T Zellmer named ADDS&T Sayre **STEVENS** becomes DDI

11.22.76 — OSI and OWI moved back to the DI from the DS&T

09.04.73 — OWI formed from merger of FMSAC and OSI/Defensive Systems Division

09.20.73 — Karl H. **WEBER** named Director, OSI

01.06.75 — Ernest (Zeke) **ZELLMER** named D/OWI

01.12.80 — Karl WEBER retires; Herbert **ROTHENBERG** named acting D/OSI

02.25.80 — OSWR formed from merger of OSI and OWI; **OSI no longer exists after 31 years**

11.1988 — New Headquarters Building opens

09.18.97 — Of the **50 original CIA Trailblazers** honored during the CIA's 50th Anniversary celebration, seven were former OSIers: Bud Wheelon, Carl Duckett, Hank Lowenhaupt, Lloyd Lauderdale, Joseph Castillo, Archie Roy Burks, and Leslie Dirks.

(1997)

CIA Trailblazers

CENTRAL INTELLIGENCE AGENCY
Washington, D.C.

31 December 1948

GENERAL ORDER
NUMBER 13

1. The revised organization charts now being distributed confirm the establishment of the Office of Scientific Intelligence, replacing the Scientific Branch of the Office of Reports and Estimates.

2. Dr. Willard Machle has been appointed as Assistant Director for Scientific Intelligence.

R. H. HILLENKOETTER
Rear Admiral, USN
Director of Central Intelligence

DISTRIBUTION: A

ANNEX "A"

C O P Y

General Order No. 13, dated 31 December 1948, established the Office with an authorized Table of Organization of ☐. This order established O/SI:

"As the primary intelligence evaluation, analysis and production component of CIA with exclusive responsibility for the production and presentation of national scientific intelligence:

"1. Prepares scientific intelligence reports and estimates designed to present and interpret the status, progress and significance of foreign scientific research and developments which affect the capabilities and potentials of all foreign nations.

"2. Makes substantive review of basic scientific intelligence produced by other agencies and advises ORE on its adequacy for inclusion in the National Intelligence Surveys.

"3. Participates in the formulation of the National Scientific Intelligence Objectives.

"4. Evaluates available scientific intelligence information and intelligence; assesses its adequacy, accuracy, and timeliness, and prepares reports of such assessments for the guidance of collection, source exploitation and producing agencies to assure that all significant fields of scientific intelligence bearing on the National security are adequately covered.

"5. Formulates requirements for the collection and exploitation of scientific intelligence data in order to insure receipt of materials necessary for fulfillment of production requirements.

"6. In collaboration with appropriate CIA components and the IAC agencies, advises and aids in the development, coordination and execution of the overall plans and policies for inter-agency scientific intelligence production."

C O P Y

The Office of Scientific Intelligence, 1949-68

I. <u>Background</u>

WW II saw the first stirrings of U.S. intelligence interest in the scientific and technical capabilities of foreign countries. Largely under the impetus of German development of radar, missiles and diverse weapons-related technologies, the separate armed services and various committees of the Office of Scientific Research and Development (OSRD) became customers for scientific and technical intelligence on foreign activities. In these wartime years information on such subjects was most often obtained through combat intelligence and the exploitation of captured materiel, with occasional assists from clandestine and intercept operations. British success in fathoming German secret weapons programs contributed to the awakening of interest in U.S. official circles.

In the early 40s, however, no discrete U.S. organization could be labeled an "office of scientific intelligence". Scientific and technical intelligence was more an offshoot of the interests of the research and development (R&D) elements than an entity in its own right. In rather distinct contrast, the British had an identifiable unit under Dr. R. V. Jones in the

- 1 -

Intelligence Branch, Air Ministry which played a major role in the wartime efforts against German aircraft and secret weapons programs.

One exception to this general state of affairs in the U.S. was a foreign intelligence unit, the Foreign Intelligence Branch, in the Manhattan Engineering District (MED), the wartime agency under General Leslie Groves concerned with nuclear weapons development. It may be recalled that considerable fear was felt in some quarters, as the feasibility of nuclear weapons seemed increasingly assured, that the Germans might be carrying on a nuclear weapons program. It was reasoned that the early experiments on atomic fission had been performed by Germans, notably the Nobel Prize winners Otto Hahn and Lisa Meitner, and hence German understanding of the underlying principles of nuclear weapons was as great as ours. Attempts to establish the existence of a German program through clandestine operations were not altogether reassuring. Anxiety continued throughout the war in the West and even into the final stages of the war against Japan.

At the close of the war, while the soul-searching into the Pearl Harbor disaster was taking place, the assets of the Office of Strategic Services (OSS) were transferred in 1946 to an interim agency, the Central

Intelligence Group (CIG), under the general surveillance of a National Intelligence Authority. This was the first attempt to consolidate and centralize the highest level intelligence functions of the U.S. Government.

In CIG the analytical functions were centered in the Office of Research and Evaluation (ORE).* Under the persistent urging of the Joint Research and Development Board (JRDB),** the peace-time successor to the OSRD ▓▓ Through an agreement between General Groves and General Hoyt S. Vandenberg, the Director of the CIG, the Foreign Intelligence Branch of MED was transferred to

---

*The Office of Research and Evaluation, organized 22 July 1946, was renamed the Office of Reports and Estimates on 27 October of the same year.

**Eventually an agreement, entitled "Program for JRDB-CIG cooperation in the field of scientific intelligence," was signed by Gen. Hoyt S. Vandenberg and Dr. Vannevar Bush on 10 January 1947. The agreement followed much discussion and investigation by JRDB. It was perhaps the first high-level recognition of the desirability of combining intelligence considerations with scientific and military factors in the planning of weapons R&D in the U.S.

the CIG on 25 February 1947 and assigned to the [redacted] [redacted] by order of the DDCI on 28 March 1947. [redacted]

As might be expected, [redacted] was seriously hampered by lack of experienced personnel. Of equal importance, it also lacked sources of information and there is evidence to suggest that its support from top management was less than vigorous. [redacted]

Despite these shortcomings of the [redacted] the JRDB persisted in its demands for intelligence support during 1946-47 and into early 1948 with [redacted] and Ralph L. Clark* as the two most outspoken advocates.

In its testimony before the Eberstadt Committee of the Hoover Commission* in 1948, the JRDB voiced its general dissatisfaction with the intelligence support it was receiving. Prompted by this view, which one can imagine was presented with vigor by Dr. Bush (Chairman, RDB) backed up by Ralph Clark, the Eberstadt Committee in turn expressed its view as follows:

> "The Committee is particularly concerned over the nation's inadequacies in the fields of scientific and medical intelligence. There are difficulties peculiar to this situation which the Committee has not overlooked. Yet the vital importance of reliable and up-to-date scientific and medical information is such as to call for far greater efforts than appear to have been devoted to this essential need in the past."

Persistent JRDB prodding of CIG and CIA may well have been the most important external pressure leading to the eventual establishment of OSI.

With the passage of the National Security Act of 1947 and the creation of the CIA, the heretofore uncertain responsibilities of the CIG gave way to the statutorily defined mission of a greatly strengthened and centralized intelligence service, the CIA. The change to a more encompassing role for CIA and the growing capabilities of the military intelligence

---

* More properly named the Committee on the National Security Organization of the Commission on Reorganization of the Executive Branch of the Government.

agencies prompted Admiral Hillenkoetter, who had succeeded General Vandenberg, to ask Dr. Bush in 1948 whether the old JRDB-CIG agreement should not be supplanted. Bush's reply was both assent and complaint for he felt that the Agency had never really begun to satisfy JRDB's needs. He agreed, however, in a letter of 26 March 1948 to set aside the formal agreement.

In particular, the coordinating and estimate producing functions of the new Agency were more firmly rooted and its resources greatly increased over those of the old. More or less concurrently, the period of uncertainty about the true intentions of the USSR and its threat to the U.S. ended. Doubts about the reality of a U.S. monopoly in nuclear weapons were fed by reports of Soviet interest in the advanced technology acquired from the Germans. There was an increasing sense of urgency about strengthening the U.S. intelligence posture.

At about the same time as the Eberstadt Committee was making its review for the Hoover Commission in 1948 another and separate review was being conducted for the National Security Council (NSC) by a team consisting of Allen W. Dulles, William H. Jackson, and Mathias F. Correa. The latter investigation resulted in the so-called Dulles Report of 1 January 1949 which had this to say about scientific intelligence:

> "We believe that there is an obvious need for more centralization of scientific intelligence. Where centralization is not practical there should be the closest coordination among the existing agencies through the use of committees such as the present interdepartmental atomic energy intelligence committee which works in consultation with the ▢▢▢▢▢ of the Office of Special Operations (. . .). A strong ▢▢▢▢▢ as a common service within the Central Intelligence Agency, would be the logical focal point for the coordination and appropriate centralization of scientific intelligence. There appears to be no overriding reason for the segregation of the ▢▢▢▢▢ within the Office of Special Operations, and it would be preferable to reattach this Group to the ▢▢▢▢▢ even though some insulation may be necessary for security reasons."*
>
> "To fulfill its responsibilities as the chief analytical and evaluating unit for scientific intelligence, and consequently as the principal guide for collection, the Branch would have to be staffed by scientists of the highest qualifications. We appreciate that in such a Branch it would be impossible to obtain a leading scientist for each of the many segments of scientific and technological intelligence,

---

*We understand that since this report was written steps have been taken to create a separate Office of Scientific Intelligence which is to include the ▢▢▢▢▢ (Author's Note: The foregoing sentence was a footnote to the Dulles Report. NSC approval of the portions of the Dulles Report dealing with the strengthening of scientific intelligence did not come until 7 July 1949. CIA in the meantime had moved to establish OSI without waiting for NSC action.)

- 7 -

but we believe that a staff of moderate size and of high quality can cope with the normal research and evaluation, co-opting, where necessary, personnel from such organizations as the Research and Development Board and the Atomic Energy Commission."

Under the impetus of the Hoover Commission and Dulles reports, the pressure on CIA and the DOD to get on with scientific intelligence mounted. The way was paved for a stronger CIA scientific intelligence effort.

II. Establishment of OSI and The Machle Period, 1949-50

A major reorganization of CIA took place in 1948 under the tenure of the then DCI, Admiral Roscoe Hillenkoetter. The process of splitting up the former ORE, which contained political, economic, and scientific units, among others, was begun.*

The activation date for OSI was 1 January 1949.

---
*In time not only OSI but also the Office of Research and Reports (economic, basic and geographic), the Office of Collection and Dissemination (forerunner of OCR), the Office of National Estimates, the Office of Current Intelligence, and the Office of Intelligence Coordination emerged.

**See Annex I.

OSI and NIE Program

UNCLASSIFIED

1 July 1952

MEMORANDUM FOR THE DEPUTY DIRECTOR/INTELLIGENCE [Becker]

SUBJECT: The Problem of Scientific and Technical Intelligence

1. Herewith some thoughts on the problem of scientific and technical intelligence which are pretty close to convictions with me.

2. Without in any way trying to derogate the importance and the extraordinary difficulty of your administrative problems, let me repeat that had O/NE not had the assistance of O/SI in drafting ████████████ that estimate would have been a quite different and far, far less useful document. In fact, it is my belief that without O/SI's interpretation of the evidence and with no corrective for service interpretation of the evidence, C/NE could have done nothing but accept the service interpretation which in the light of what I learned from C/SI would have been an over-reassuring one.

3. Obviously this is for your private eye and just as obviously if I give it any further circulation it will be to Washington Platt on an "Eyes Only" basis.

SHERMAN KENT
Assistant Director
National Estimates

This document has been approved for release through the HISTORICAL REVIEW PROGRAM of the Central Intelligence Agency.

Date 1/25/91
HRP 89-2

SECRET

UNCLASSIFIED

SOME THOUGHTS ON THE PROBLEM OF SCIENTIFIC AND TECHNICAL INTELLIGENCE

1. In any country's security system there are elements upon which the country in question places great store. These are truly its secrets of security.

2. Generally speaking these secrets of security if they are not in themselves scientific and technical at least rest on scientific and technological developments. Ask yourself: Knowledge of what twenty US secrets of security would I be most concerned to keep from the USSR? How many of the twenty really lie outside the scientific/technical area?

3. The importance which a country attaches to any of these elements in its security system is an index of that country's desire to keep them secret from all outsiders. Thus the more important they are the more difficult they become as intelligence targets.

4. The security measures in operation in the USSR have been peculiarly successful in the scientific/technical area. It would be my guess that in no part of our knowledge of Soviet secrets of security is the ratio of fixed points to voids so large. In the matter of the gadgets around which Soviet air defense capabilities are built, the paucity of fixed points is dramatic in the extreme.

5. In the last analysis the mission of intelligence is to draw the meaningful and objective generalization from the data.

   a. If the data, or fixed points, are numerous and the voids between them small, then meaningful, objective, and probably correct generalizations can be drawn.

   b. If the data, or fixed points, are few and the voids between them large, meaningful generalizations can still be drawn. But who is to say that they are objective and/or probably correct? Who is to say they are anything but mere fiction?

- 2 -

6. In case 5b above, the generalizer, minimally confined and directed by fixed points, may be engulfed by forces wholly extraneous to the problem at hand. It is here that he may be consciously or unconsciously taken over by his hopes, his wishes, and his fears, or by those of his friends or the institution he works for. (I refer you to the men who have designed maps of the heavens and who have generalized the muscular Orion and his club, belt, and lion skin from a dozen or so stars.) What he comes up with is something far different from and usually far more or less than the meager suggestions of the fixed points. The added something is not from the data; it is from him.

7. As long as the national intelligence community can fix only relatively few points in key scientific and technical developments of the USSR and as long as the voids between these points are very large, generalizations by any single individual or single intelligence institution may be dangerously skewed by individual wish or institution policy.

8. Ask yourself: "What would I wish if my future were interwoven with that of one of the armed services?" You would wish to be a part of the best damn outfit of its sort in existence — an outfit that could deliver enough lethal power to destroy any enemy in a single attack and do it without losing a man.

9. Ask yourself the next question: "What do I do to get my wish?" If you are in intelligence you may do two things.

   a. To assure yourself that your service will get the funds to make it the best damn outfit of its sort in existence you will not play down the enemy. You will build him up, especially in gross terms of his offensive capability.

   b. To assure yourself that once you've got the best damn outfit in the world, it will carry out its mission you begin to take away from the enemy. You will take away notably in the area of his defensive capabilities. You are not quite so certain to do this as to build up his offensive capabilities, because of the perils involved. You know that if you significantly undervalue his defensive capabilities and plans are drawn upon your

- 3 -

evaluation your service may be cruelly hurt in the clash. You finally fix the point of his defensive capabilities at the place where the curve of your wish intersects the curve of your fear. The fixed points are so few that you can easily draw your curves to accommodate them.

10. When you have done these two things you have done little more than describe the ideal enemy: the enemy big enough to warrant the perfection of your outfit, but an enemy who is nevertheless a push-over in a showdown.

11. You can do this in the field of scientific and technical intelligence on the USSR, and no one can say you may so long as the ratio of fixed points to voids remains what it is.

12. The above is a long way of spelling out my doubts as to the virtues of assigning to given departmental intelligence organisations a "primary" responsibility in any of the specific areas of scientific and technical intelligence. All along I have feared the generalisations, say, that ONI may make of the fixed points and voids re Soviet underwater warfare techniques, that G-2 may make re Soviet tank design, that A-2 may make re Soviet GCI and A-2 radar and AAA. I have however been somewhat comforted by realising that if any single service comes up with a wishful generalisation, this generalization may be opposed to the wish of another service; that the other service will possess all the data of the first and that it will be capable of drawing its own variant or opposing generalization.

13. If a service is duly invested with "primary" responsibility and if at the same time it possesses sources of information which it may or may not share with other services and if it chooses not to share, the chances of another service developing a variant or opposing generalization have shrunk considerably and may have shrunk to approximate zero.

14. We are in a position today where we cannot anticipate either (a) a dramatic decrease in the ratio of voids to fixed points in the area of scientific and technical developments in the USSR or (b) a dramatic change in human nature. As long as

- 4 -

we do not take out insurance against the acceptance of a generalization that must perforce partake heavily of the wish, we are asking for trouble. If I were carrying the statutory responsibilities of the DCI the minimum insurance I would take out would be as follows:

   a. Keep O/SI in business pretty much as it is today -- even endeavor to strengthen some of its divisions. The ones I would strengthen would be those dealing with the most important subject matter irrespective of whether another agency had been awarded "primary" responsibility in this subject matter.

   b. Set up a machinery to insure that no one scientific/technical intelligence outfit withheld information which it may have developed and which it found useful in drawing its own generalizations.

NATIONAL INTELLIGENCE ESTIMATE

SOVIET BLOC CAPABILITIES THROUGH 1957

**CIA HISTORICAL REVIEW PROGRAM
RELEASE IN FULL**

NIE-65

Approved 9 June 1953

Published 16 June 1953

The Intelligence Advisory Committee concurred in this estimate on 9 June 1953. The FBI abstained, the subject being outside of its jurisdiction.

The following member organizations of the Intelligence Advisory Committee participated with the Central Intelligence Agency in the preparation of this estimate: The intelligence organizations of the Departments of State, the Army, the Navy, the Air Force, and the Joint Staff.

CENTRAL INTELLIGENCE AGENCY

SERIES _____

COPY _____ OF _____

SOVIET BLOC CAPABILITIES THROUGH 1957

THE PROBLEM

To analyze the principal factors affecting Soviet Bloc capabilities and to estimate the probable development of those capabilities, through 1957.

ASSUMPTION

That there will not be general war within the period of this estimate.

CONCLUSIONS

1. Developments within the USSR resulting from the change in leadership may ultimately affect Soviet Bloc capabilities, but so far the economic and military bases of Soviet power are believed not to have been affected by Stalin's death. This estimate, therefore, is based on the trends within the Soviet Bloc since 1945, and does not attempt to estimate whether, or to what extent, these trends may be affected by changes within the ruling group.[1]

[1] The Special Assistant, Intelligence, Department of State, the Assistant Chief of Staff, G-2, Intelligence, Department of the Army, and the Deputy Director for Intelligence, The Joint Staff, believe that this sentence should be replaced with the following:

It is impossible as yet to estimate with confidence whether or not a prolonged struggle for power among the new leaders will develop during the period 1953-1957. We believe, however, that if such a struggle for power should develop, it would be confined to the higher echelons of the Soviet Communist Party and Government and would probably not precipitate open conflict within or between the armed forces and security police, or involve the Soviet population. We estimate, therefore, that the stability of the regime in the USSR is unlikely to be jeopardized by differences that may develop among the Soviet leaders.

2. The rate of growth of the Soviet economy will almost certainly remain higher than that of the US or any other major Western state. However, the output of the USSR will remain much lower than that of the US, and the output of the entire Bloc will remain much lower than that of the NATO states.

3. Bloc scientific and technical capabilities will continue to increase throughout the period of this estimate. However, the scientific assets (the number and quality of trained personnel, facilities, equipment, and financial support) of the US will remain greater than those of the USSR, and the assets of the West as a whole will remain far greater than those of the Bloc.

4. By mid-1957, the USSR may have a stockpile of from 335 to 1,000 atomic weapons (30-100 kiloton yield).[2] We have no evidence that *thermonuclear* weapons are being developed by the

[2] The estimates beyond mid-1955 are tentative projections of the estimates for the earlier years.

USSR. Soviet research, development, and even field testing of thermonuclear reactions based on the disclosures of Fuchs may take place by mid-1953. However, it is very unlikely that the USSR could test a full scale thermonuclear device based on these disclosures before mid-1954. There is also a possibility that Soviet field tests based on independent research and development along other and advanced approaches to the thermonuclear weapons problem might occur by mid-1954. Testing of advanced models might be possible earlier if US developments were known through espionage or other compromise.

5. The USSR now has the capability seriously to disrupt Western long-range radio communications and navigation systems.[3] Soviet capabilities in related electronic fields indicate that the USSR is now capable of developing equipment for jamming frequencies up through SHF, and the USSR could produce such equipment by 1957. If such equipment were produced on a large scale and placed in operational use, it would probably constitute a threat to Western short-range radio communications, navigation, and, to a lesser extent, bombing systems, unless Western anti-jamming capabilities were improved.

6. We estimate that the size of Bloc forces-in-being will not increase substantially by 1957. The emphasis in the program for increasing Bloc military strength will continue to be placed upon modernizing the armed forces and upon enlarging the atomic stockpile.

[3] For more detailed information, see SE-38, "Soviet Bloc Capabilities and Probable Courses of Action in Electromagnetic Warfare" (24 April 1953).

7. We estimate that the Bloc now has the capability to undertake[4] concurrent large-scale operations in continental Europe, the Middle East, and mainland Asia. The Bloc could reinforce with Chinese Communist and Soviet forces the Communist forces now in Korea, and at the same time undertake[4] an invasion of Japan by Soviet forces.

8. The USSR now has the capability to undertake[4] concurrent air operations against the US, the UK, continental Europe, the Middle East, Japan, and the offshore island chain of Asia. However, operations against the US would be much more difficult than those against the other areas. The USSR has the capability to reach all parts of the US and to attempt the delivery of its full stockpile of atomic weapons. However, even a stripped-down TU-4 could reach only the extreme northwestern corner on two-way missions without aerial refueling. Even with aerial refueling and other range extension techniques,[5] attack upon the strategic northeastern industrial area and upon most of the principal strategic bases almost certainly would involve the expenditure of the attacking aircraft and most of the crews on one-way missions. Until it has a heavy bomber available for operational use, the USSR will not have the capability to reach most of the strategically important areas in the US on two-way missions. A heavy bomber based upon a type which has been seen in flight

[4] No estimate of the success of these operations can be made without considering the effects of the actions of opposing forces.

[5] We believe that the USSR has the capability to utilize range extension techniques, but we have no evidence that any of these techniques have been exploited.

may be in production and may be available for operational use within the period of this estimate.[6]

9. We estimate that the Bloc has the capability of providing vigorous opposition against air attacks on critical targets in the interior of the USSR, under conditions of good visibility. Under clear moonlit night conditions, Bloc defense capabilities are fair against piston bombers and negligible against jet bombers. Under conditions of poor visibility, day or night, Bloc interception capabilities are negligible.

10. Currently known trends point to an increase of Bloc air defense capabilities during the period of this estimate. However, it is impossible to estimate the extent of significance of any increase, because the future development of airborne intercept (AI) equipment and of guided missiles is obscure; in any case, such an estimate would require knowledge of the characteristics of attacking aircraft through the period of this estimate.[7]

11. Bloc naval forces (except for ocean-going submarines, and new cruisers and destroyers) as now constituted are designed to protect Bloc coastal areas and seaward flanks of ground campaigns. We believe that, as new construction with improved characteristics becomes operational, emphasis will be laid on the creation of striking forces which could operate within the limits of the range of land-based air support. Bloc minelaying capability is extensive, and in the event of war, could seriously interfere with Allied sea communications in Europe and the Far East, or with Western naval operations in waters adjacent to the USSR. The Soviet submarine force will increase its capability to undertake offensive patrols and mining operations along most of the world's strategically vital sea lanes, and possibly, if the specialized craft have been developed, simultaneously to launch guided missile attacks against targets on both the Atlantic and Pacific seaboards of the US.[8] The Soviet Navy will have no long-range amphibious capabilities within the period of this estimate, but it will remain capable of mounting short-range amphibious operations in considerable force.

12. The principal sources of strength upon which Bloc political warfare capabilities are based will remain Bloc military power, which generates fear and defeatism, and the Bloc's size, strategic position, economic power and potential, and centralized direction. Other sources of Bloc political warfare strength are the highly organized Communist international movement, and the leadership and discipline of the individual Communist

---

[6] For more detailed information, see SE-36, "Soviet Capabilities for Attacks on the US through Mid-1955" (5 March 1953).

[7] The Director of Naval Intelligence believes that this paragraph should read as follows:
We believe the Bloc will continue its present emphasis on air defense, and that its capabilities in this respect will increase during the period of this estimate. Operational use of improved early warning and ground intercept radar, and the extensive employment of airborne intercept equipment will contribute to this increase. The development and production of all-weather jet fighters and guided missiles, which are within Bloc capabilities, would further improve Bloc air defense. However, we cannot estimate the significance of these improvements relative to future air offensive capabilities.

[8] We believe the USSR capable of adapting submarines to this use, but we have no evidence to indicate that such modifications have been made.

Parties; Communist ideas and doctrine, which influence many non-Communists as well as Communists; and the accumulated experience and professional skill of Soviet intelligence, propaganda, and subversive organizations and of Soviet use of front organizations. Finally, the fixity of Communist purpose to impose Communism on the world and the unified direction of Communist action give the Communists a tactical political warfare advantage in determining the nature, direction, and intensity of courses of action to be used against the non-Communist world.

13. It is difficult to estimate how Bloc political warfare capabilities will develop, since they depend to a large degree not only upon the situation within the USSR but also upon the success with which the non-Communist world meets the challenges to its stability which would exist even if there were no Communist threat. It is also difficult to estimate the development of Bloc political warfare capabilities because they are dependent not only on the relative attractive power of Communist and non-Communist ideas, but on the relative military strength of the Bloc and the West. If Western military strength should increase, relative to that of the Bloc, Bloc political warfare capabilities would probably decline. On the other hand, fear of war and consequent vulnerability to Bloc political warfare would probably increase in the non-Communist world, if the Bloc's capability to deliver atomic weapons should increase relative to Western defenses, and if the Bloc should improve its air defenses relative to Western offensive capabilities.[9]

14. We believe that during the period of this estimate Communist capabilities to establish Communist governments by political warfare techniques will be most likely to increase in Southeast Asia and the Middle East. These capabilities will probably remain greatest in Iran and Indochina.

15. In other areas of the world, Communist capabilities to influence the attitudes of non-Communist governments and peoples will constitute the principal danger posed by Bloc political warfare. The Communists may be able to undermine support for Western programs of defense and for increased political and economic unity, and they may be able to heighten tensions among the members of the Western coalition. For these purposes, they can exploit national differences between the Western Powers, economic and trade difficulties, nationalism in colonial and dependent areas, and dread of war.

---

[9] The Director of Naval Intelligence believes this paragraph should read as follows in order to render the military hypothesis more realistic and inclusive:

It is difficult to estimate how Bloc political warfare capabilities will develop, since they depend to a large degree upon the situation within the USSR, the success with which the non-Communist world meets the challenges to its stability which would exist even if there were no Communist threat, and the relative military strengths of the Bloc and the West. Thus, Bloc political warfare capabilities will increase if the non-Communist world fails to solve adequately the problems of economic stability, national rivalries, common defense, and aspirations for independence in the colonial areas. If Western military strength and cohesion should increase substantially relative to that of the Bloc, Bloc political warfare capabilities would probably be checked, and might decline in some areas. On the other hand, if the over-all military strength of the Bloc should substantially increase relative to that of the West, Bloc political warfare capabilities would rise, particularly with respect to the promotion of appeasement, apathy, and the fear of war.

~~TOP SECRET~~
U.S. OFFICIALS ONLY

Copy No. 67

NATIONAL INTELLIGENCE ESTIMATE

SUMMARY
THE SOVIET ATOMIC ENERGY PROGRAM TO MID-1957

**CIA HISTORICAL REVIEW PROGRAM
RELEASE IN FULL**

NIE 11–3A–54
16 February 1954

The Intelligence Advisory Committee concurred in this estimate on 16 February 1954. The FBI abstained, the subject being outside of its jurisdiction.

The following member organizations of the Intelligence Advisory Committee participated with the Central Intelligence Agency in the preparation of this estimate: The intelligence organizations of the Departments of State, the Army, the Navy, the Air Force, the Joint Staff, and the Atomic Energy Commission.

CENTRAL INTELLIGENCE AGENCY

SERIES _____
COPY _____ OF _____

~~TOP SECRET~~
U.S. OFFICIALS ONLY

NATIONAL INTELLIGENCE ESTIMATE

JOINT ATOMIC ENERGY INTELLIGENCE COMMITTEE

SUMMARY

THE SOVIET ATOMIC ENERGY PROGRAM
TO MID-1957

NIE 11-3A-54

16 February 1954

This is a summary of National Intelligence Estimate, NIE 11-3-54, dated 16 February 1954, prepared and agreed upon by the Joint Atomic Energy Intelligence Committee which is composed of representatives of the Departments of State, Army, Navy, Air Force, the Atomic Energy Commission, the Joint Staff and the Central Intelligence Agency. The FBI abstained, the subject being outside of its jurisdiction.

A group of expert consultants working with the Joint Atomic Energy Intelligence Committee concurred in the conclusions given in this estimate. The estimate was approved by the Intelligence Advisory Committee as of 16 February 1954.

SUMMARY
THE SOVIET ATOMIC ENERGY PROGRAM
TO MID-1957

THE PROBLEM

To estimate the current status and future course of the Soviet atomic energy program on the basis of information available from all sources.

SUMMARY

1. While the exact extent of the Soviet capability for quantity production of nuclear weapons remains uncertain in some of its aspects, the available evidence establishes the existence in the USSR of (a) a high-priority, extensive atomic energy program; (b) a substantial stockpile of nuclear weapons; and (c) the capability of producing explosions in a range from the equivalent of a few thousand to at least a million tons of TNT.

2. In November 1945 the "First Chief Directorate attached to the Council of Ministers" was organized to plan and carry out the Soviet atomic energy program.

3. The first Soviet reactor capable of quantity production of plutonium probably went into operation during 1948 and by the spring and summer of 1949 the level of total reactor power became significant, thus marking the date of the start of production scale operations for the manufacture of plutonium.

4. The production of uranium-235 apparently lagged behind the plutonium program. Whether this was planned or the result of technical difficulties is not known, as only meager evidence is available that is relevant to the isotope separation phase of the program.

5. The Soviets have demonstrated a capability to accomplish independent research essential to their atomic energy program. While it is no doubt true that espionage activities, German technical assistance, and unclassified scientific and technical literature available in Western countries made substantial contributions to Soviet progress, independent research by the Soviets, required to adapt to their needs the information obtained through such sources, was apparently carried out with a high degree of competence. The evidence is now clear that in a number of instances Soviet atomic energy practices do not follow those of the U.S., the U.K. or Canada.

6. It is estimated that the total cumulative production of uranium metal available to the Soviet Union from East German production alone up to the end of 1953 was between 10 and 15 thousand tons. It is possible that an equal amount could have been produced from internal and other Satellite sources.

7. The Soviets are depending, for the most part, on very low-grade deposits of uranium. In the Satellites the major portion of the uranium recovered is derived from ores which probably average between 0.03% and 0.3% U_3O_8. Only a vast amount of hand sorting can account for the large output. Comparable grades of ore are probably being extensively worked inside the USSR.

8. It is estimated that the probable total reactor power levels were in the neighborhood of 900 - 1200 megawatts during the period from early 1952 to the end of 1953. Further, it is estimated the total effective reactor power levels will increase during the period of this estimate, reaching a level of approximately 2100 to 2400 megawatts in 1957. It should be noted that this increase is not intended to define the maximum capability for expansion of Soviet plutonium manufacturing facilities.

9. The absence of sufficient evidence from which to estimate installed or planned isotope separation capacity continues to be one of the most serious gaps in intelligence information on the Soviet atomic energy program. It is believed that there are several possible courses of action the Soviets may have taken with respect to uranium-235 production which are consistent with available evidence and which yield general guide lines for the Soviet uranium-235 stockpile. An average value has been taken for the purpose of calculating the weapons stockpile.

10. No evidence is available on Soviet efforts with respect to power applications of atomic energy other than possible implications from Soviet interest in thorium and the high irradiation level of the plutonium utilized in the 3 September 1953 explosion. However, together with continuing research on methods of plutonium and uranium-233 production, some effort will undoubtedly be placed on power applications.

11. It is concluded that the USSR is capable of producing nuclear weapons with explosive powers in the range of the equivalent of a few thousand tons of TNT to approximately one million tons of TNT. Throughout this range thermonuclear reactions were apparently used to increase (i.e. boost) the energy yield from the fissionable materials present without themselves directly contributing substantially to the total energy yield. It is apparent that by the end of 1953 the Soviets had reached a point in weapon technology at which they were capable of producing stockpile weapon types dictated by military requirements.

- 2 -

12. While there is no clear evidence which can serve as a guide to an estimate of the specific types and numbers of each type that the Soviets will actually stockpile, it is considered probable that for the immediate future the specific weapons stockpiled will have the general characteristics and explosive powers of models tested. However, as estimates are projected further into the future, uncertainty is increased by the possible advent of new principles of weapon design or the development of new methods for the production of fissionable or thermonuclear materials.

13. In order to illustrate how estimated Soviet stockpiles of fissionable materials may be utilized, the table below has been based upon two examples of the many courses which are within Soviet capabilities: (a) the continued stockpiling of composite and pure plutonium weapons using principles tested in 1951 and yielding approximately the equivalent of 40,000 tons of TNT each, or (b) the stockpiling of nuclear weapons using the boosting principles tested in 1953, i.e. utilization of plutonium components for medium yield (60,000 tons of TNT) and small yield (5,000 tons of TNT) weapons, and all uranium-235 weapons yielding one million tons of TNT.

Stockpile Examples	End 1953	Mid-1954	Mid-1955	Mid-1956	Mid-1957
(a) Unboosted composite and plutonium weapons 40 KT each	180	240	390	575	800
Total yield (million tons TNT)	7.2	9.6	15.6	23	32
or					
(b) Boosted uranium or plutonium weapons 1000 KT	12	18	34	54	80
60 KT	60	85	125	175	235
5 KT	190	250	375	525	700
Total yield (million tons TNT)	16.5	24.3	43.4	65.6	97.5

14. For comparison with the above, the following table sets forth the stockpile figures which would be applicable if the Soviets fabricated all fissionable material into either large-yield boosted weapons (e.g. uranium-235 weapons yielding 1000 kilotons each, and pure plutonium weapons yielding 60 kilotons each) or small-yield weapons (e.g. composite and pure plutonium weapons yielding 5 kilotons each).

UNCLASSIFIED

5 October 1954

NATIONAL INTELLIGENCE ESTIMATE
NUMBER 11-6-54

SOVIET CAPABILITIES AND PROBABLE PROGRAMS IN THE GUIDED MISSILE FIELD

**CIA HISTORICAL REVIEW PROGRAM
RELEASE IN FULL**

BEST COPY AVAILABLE

UNCLASSIFIED

SOVIET CAPABILITIES AND PROBABLE PROGRAMS IN THE GUIDED MISSILE FIELD

THE PROBLEM

To estimate Soviet capabilities and probable programs in the field of guided missiles.

FOREWORD

In preparing this estimate we have had available conclusive evidence of a great postwar Soviet interest in guided missiles and indications that the USSR has a large and active research and development program. However, we have no firm current intelligence on what particular guided missiles the USSR is presently developing or may now have in operational use. Therefore, in order to estimate specific Soviet missile capabilities we have been forced to reason from: (a) the available evidence of Soviet missile activity, including exploitation of German missile experience; (b) our own guided missile experience; and (c) estimated Soviet capabilities in related fields. In addition, we have analyzed such factors as: (a) Soviet industrial resources and economic capabilities; (b) Soviet nuclear capabilities in relation to guided missiles; (c) the estimated reliability of missile systems; (d) various logistic and training factors; and (e) Soviet capabilities in geodesy and cartography. Finally, in the absence of current evidence on specific Soviet missile projects, we have estimated Soviet intentions on the basis of probable Soviet military requirements, within the context of probable Soviet capabilities in this and other weapons fields. Therefore our estimates of missile characteristics and of dates of missile availability must be considered as only tentative, and as representing our best assessment in the light of inadequate evidence and in a new and largely unexplored field.

CONCLUSIONS

GENERAL CONCLUSIONS

1. We believe that the strategic requirements of the USSR would dictate a major effort in the field of guided missiles, and the evidence which we have concerning large number of personalities and activities believed to be involved in the current Soviet missile program leads us to the conclusion that it is an extensive one. However, our evidence is insufficient to permit a more precise estimate as to the magnitude of this program.

2. On the basis of our extensive knowledge of Soviet exploitation of the wartime German missile experience and our estimate of Soviet capabilities in related fields, we believe that the USSR has the basic scientific and technical capabilities

to support a comprehensive missile research and development program.

3. The USSR also has an adequate economic base for a sizeable missile production program. However, because of the limited capabilities of the Soviet electronics and precision mechanisms industries and other competing demands for their output, the USSR will almost certainly be unable to produce in the desired quantities all of the missiles for which it has an estimated military requirement, except over an extended period of years. Consequently, the USSR will probably concentrate over the next few years on those missiles for which it has the most urgent military requirements.

4. Over the next several years the increasing size of the Soviet nuclear stockpile and the larger yields estimated to be available from nuclear warheads will make missiles an increasingly practicable means of nuclear attack, despite their limitations in reliability and accuracy.[1] Nevertheless, because of these limitations we believe that the Soviets will place primary reliance on aircraft delivery of nuclear weapons so long as the Soviet stockpile remains limited and Allied air defenses can be penetrated without unacceptable losses. We recognize, however, that these considerations would not preclude earlier employment of nuclear missiles when the advantages of surprise or other factors so dictate.

5. Although we have no evidence to confirm or deny current Soviet missile production, we believe that the Allies will face a growing Soviet guided missile threat within the next several years. This threat will probably appear first in increased Soviet air defense capabilities, together with or followed by improved Soviet capabilities against US and Allied coastal areas and sea lines of communication and in tactical operations. Later the threat will probably extend to all Allied base areas in Eurasia, and ultimately to the entire US. The following dates for specific missile capabilities give the earliest probable dates when we estimate the threat could begin, but it should be recognized that an additional varying period of time would be required for these missiles to be available in large quantities.

SPECIFIC MISSILE CAPABILITIES

6. *Surface-to-Air Missiles.* The Soviets will probably devote highest priority to producing surface-to-air missiles to overcome their serious air defense deficiencies. We estimate that they could now have an all-weather improved Wasserfall design and in 1955[2] a further improved version

---

[1] See Annex C, *Restricted Data*, for estimates of time-phased warhead yields.

[2] The estimated dates given in this estimate are the earliest probable years during which small quantities of missiles could have been produced and placed in the hands of trained personnel of one operational unit, thus constituting a limited capability for operational employment. These dates are based on the assumption that a concerted and continuous effort began in 1948. If no major delays of any sort were encountered and an intensive effort of the highest order of priority were undertaken, the earliest possible dates of availability could be on the order of one to two years earlier, or as much as three years in the case of the "intercontinental ballistic missile." The above dates are those around which the missile could have been operationally tested and be ready for series production. However, an additional period (which would vary according to missile type) would be required before missiles could be produced in quantity and the necessary units trained and deployed. We estimate that at least an additional six months would normally be required for shift or conversion from pilot plant to series production, and an additional period to reach the planned production rate. Some 18 months to two years would probably be required for individual and unit training of each operational unit, although this period could to a considerable extent overlap the production period.

with semiactive homing. In 1957–1958 they should be capable of having a much better missile with terminal homing and 50,000 yards slant range at 60,000 feet altitude. The low yield nuclear warhead probably available for this missile in 1958 would greatly increase the kill probability.

7. *Air-to-Air Missiles*. Because of its air defense weaknesses, the USSR will probably also assign a very high priority to air-to-air missiles. We estimate that it could develop in 1955 a guided rocket with infrared homing and in 1955–1958 an improved version with greater range. However, their guidance system would permit only tail cone attacks under generally fair weather conditions at the engagement altitude. In 1958–1960 the USSR could probably have a new all-weather missile.

8. *Air-to-Surface Missiles*. The USSR also would almost certainly seek to produce in quantity any precision weapon available for effective HE antiship attacks. For this purpose it could now have available and would probably produce a rocket-propelled glide bomb, although limited to good visibility conditions. In view of its extensive bomber capabilities, we do not believe that the USSR would produce a long-range air-to-surface missile for attacks on Allied ports and bases over the next several years. In 1960, on the other hand, when we estimate that an all-weather air-to-surface missile with nuclear warhead could be ready for series production, there will probably be a high priority Soviet requirement for a weapon of this type because of the increased effectiveness of Allied air defense around key target areas.

9. *Submarine-Launched Missiles*. The USSR will almost certainly have a requirement for submarine-launched missiles for nuclear attacks on US and Allied coastal areas. It could already have available improved V-1 types with nuclear warheads. In 1955 the USSR could have ready for series production a turbo-jet pilotless aircraft[3] with improved range, speed, and accuracy, and by 1958 its nuclear warhead yield could approach compatibility with its estimated accuracy and greatly increase its effectiveness.

10. *Ground-Launched Surface-to-Surface Missiles*. The USSR could also use the above pilotless aircraft from ground-launchers. However, we believe that it would favor ballistic missiles because of their relative immunity to presently known countermeasures and their greater capability for achieving surprise. The USSR probably could have available: (a) in 1954 an elongated V-2 type with 350 nautical miles range and a CEP of two nautical miles[4] or an alternative V-2 type or native design with less range but a larger warhead and a smaller CEP; (b) in 1955 an elongated V-2 type with 500 miles range and a CEP of 2.5 miles; in 1957 (or at the earliest possible date in 1955) a single stage ballistic missile with 900 miles range and a CEP of three-four

---

[3] The Assistant Chief of Staff, G-2, Department of the Army, the Director of Naval Intelligence, and the Deputy Director for Intelligence, The Joint Staff, believe that use of the term "pilotless aircraft" to define the broad category of guided missiles which are not ballistic in principle is misleading in that it gives the impression that all such missiles are conventional aircraft which have been modified to the extent that the human pilot has been replaced by the guidance equipment and which are intended to return to their bases and land. They believe that the term "nonballistic guided missile" would more adequately describe this category of missiles and should be used in lieu of "pilotless aircraft" wherever that term occurs.

[4] CEP (Circular Probable Error) means 50 percent hits within the stated radius. All CEPs and ranges are given in nautical miles.

miles; and (d) in 1959 (or at the earliest possible date in 1957) a two stage missile with 1,300 miles range and a CEP of three-four miles.[5] However, the accuracy of all these missiles would probably be markedly inferior to that obtainable by either visual or radar bombing, and their range is inferior to that of Soviet bombers. Therefore, until Allied air defenses improve greatly, we believe that the USSR will rely primarily on high performance bombers, except for all-weather use in the ground battle.

11. In view of growing Allied tactical nuclear capabilities in Europe, the USSR will probably give high priority to a ballistic missile for support of its field forces. Aside from this missile, Soviet efforts over the next several years will probably be concentrated more on ballistic missile development than upon quantity production. When the USSR estimates that improved Allied air defenses will soon pose a major threat to successful delivery by aircraft, it will probably undertake a heavy investment in these missiles. However, the limited nuclear yields now available from such warheads and the limited accuracy and reliability of these missiles point toward use of aircraft as a better means of delivery at least until 1958. Moreover, by this time estimated increases in the Soviet nuclear stockpile and in nuclear warhead yields should have greatly reduced the significance of the limitations of missile accuracy or reliability.

12. *Intercontinental Ballistic Missile (IBM)*. We believe that the USSR, looking forward to a period, possibly in the next few years, when long-range bombers may no longer be a feasible means of attacking heavily defended US targets, will make a concerted effort to produce an IBM. In this event it probably could have ready for series production in about 1963 (or at the earliest possible date in 1960) an IBM with a high yield nuclear warhead and a CEP of roughly five nautical miles.[6] Advent of the IBM would create an entirely new type of threat to the US. Attacks upon the launching sites are the only countermeasures now known or in prospect. If the USSR should develop such a missile and produce it in considerable numbers before the US developed adequate counterweapons or countermeasures, the USSR would acquire such a military advantage as to constitute an extremely grave threat to US security.

DISCUSSION

I. SOVIET SCIENTIFIC AND TECHNICAL RESOURCES

Basic Soviet Scientific and Technical Capabilities

13. *Trained Manpower*. The rising general level of technical ability in the USSR and the increasing number of scientists and engineers available provide the manpower potential necessary to staff a large guided missile program.

At the end of World War II, the USSR had an acute shortage of trained manpower and to help alleviate this condition brought about 3,500 German scientists and technicians to the USSR. Beginning at the same time, graduations from Soviet science and engineering institutions were greatly increased,

---

[5] See footnote to paragraph 6.

[6] See footnote to paragraph 6, but note that in the case of the IBM, operational firing of limited numbers might be conducted by factory technicians at the assembly site, and the full 18 months to two-year training period for missile units would not be required.

~~TOP SECRET~~

032823

NATIONAL INTELLIGENCE ESTIMATE
NUMBER 11-12-55

(Supplement, NIE 11-6-54)

SOVIET GUIDED MISSILE CAPABILITIES AND PROBABLE PROGRAMS

**CIA HISTORICAL REVIEW PROGRAM
RELEASE IN FULL**

Submitted by the
DIRECTOR OF CENTRAL INTELLIGENCE

The following intelligence organizations participated in the preparation of this estimate: The Central Intelligence Agency and the intelligence organizations of the Departments of State, the Army, the Navy, the Air Force, and The Joint Staff

Concurred in by the
INTELLIGENCE ADVISORY COMMITTEE

on 20 December 1955. Concurring were the Special Assistant, Intelligence, Department of State; the Assistant Chief of Staff, G-2, Department of the Army; the Director of Naval Intelligence; the Director of Intelligence, USAF; the Deputy Director for Intelligence, The Joint Staff; and the Atomic Energy Commission Representative to the IAC. The Assistant Director, Federal Bureau of Investigation, abstained, the subject being outside the jurisdiction of the FBI.

SERIES _____

COPY _____ OF _____

~~TOP SECRET~~   COPY NO.   293
ASSISTANT DIRECTOR, ONE

SOVIET GUIDED MISSILE CAPABILITIES AND PROBABLE PROGRAMS

THE PROBLEM

To re-estimate, wherever new evidence is available, Soviet capabilities and probable programs in the guided missile field.

FOREWORD

This estimate brings up to date and supplements, wherever new evidence was available, our previous estimate on "Soviet Capabilities and Probable Programs in the Guided Missile Field," NIE 11-6-54, dated 5 October 1954. At that time, we had no firm intelligence on specific Soviet missile capabilities. Therefore we were forced to base our specific capabilities estimates entirely on: (a) the available evidence of general Soviet missile activity, including exploitation of German missile experience; (b) extrapolation from our own guided missile experience; and (c) estimated Soviet capabilities in related fields. Similarly, our estimates of Soviet intentions had to be based on probable Soviet military requirements.

Since publication of NIE 11-6-54, new intelligence has confirmed our previous estimate that the USSR has an extensive guided missile program. The new intelligence has also changed and in some particulars strengthened our estimates of Soviet surface-to-surface and surface-to-air missile capabilities.

It is emphasized that we have no new intelligence concerning Soviet air-to-air or submarine-launched missiles, and very little new information concerning air-to-surface missiles. Our estimates in these fields therefore remain based on the analysis in NIE 11-6-54 which was necessarily speculative and in many cases based primarily on estimated Soviet requirements and US missile experience. The corresponding conclusions of NIE 11-6-54 have been carried forward into this estimate for convenience of reference only.

The dates given in this estimate are the probable years during which small quantities of missiles could have been produced and placed in the hands of trained personnel of one operational unit, thus constituting a limited capability for operational employment. These dates are based on the assumption that a concerted and continuous effort began in 1948, and are those around which the missile could have been operationally tested and be ready for series production. However, an additional period (which would vary according to missile type) would be required before missiles could be produced in quantity and the necessary units trained and deployed.

We estimate that at least an additional six months would normally be required for shift or conversion from pilot plant to series production, and an additional period to reach the planned production rate. Some 18 months to two years would probably be required for individual and unit training of each operational unit, although this period could to a considerable extent overlap the production period.

CONCLUSIONS

1. The USSR is engaged in an extensive guided missile program. We estimate that the Western Powers face a growing Soviet guided missile threat over the next several years. A threat to Western offensive capabilities is already beginning to appear in the form of increased Soviet air defense strength. This threat will probably soon be followed by improved Soviet offensive capabilities against US and Allied coastal areas and sea lines of communication, and in tactical operations. Later the threat will probably extend to all Allied base areas in Eurasia and its periphery, and ultimately to the entire US. (Paras. 9–10)

2. With the passage of time, the increasing size of the Soviet nuclear stockpile and the larger yields estimated to be available from nuclear warheads will make missiles an increasingly effective means of nuclear attack.[1] However, we believe that for the next several years the USSR would rely primarily on high performance aircraft for the delivery of nuclear weapons. Nevertheless, the advantage of surprise and other considerations might warrant earlier use of missiles with nuclear warheads for certain purposes.

SPECIFIC MISSILE CAPABILITIES

3. *Surface-to-Air Missiles.* The USSR is probably devoting very high priority to producing such missiles to overcome its air defense deficiencies. We believe that it now has deployed, at least in the Moscow area, operational surface-to-air missiles. Their performance characteristics are unknown, but might be superior to those previously estimated (see NIE 11–6–54).[2] The low yield nuclear warhead which could be available after 1958 would greatly increase their kill probability. (Paras. 11–17)

4. *Surface-to-Surface Ballistic Missiles.* Although the USSR could employ non-ballistic guided missiles from ground launchers, we believe that it would favor ballistic missiles because of their relative immunity to presently known countermeasures and their greater capability for achieving surprise. In view of growing

---

[1] See Annex A, *Restricted Data*, for estimates of time-phased warhead yields.

[2] The Assistant Chief of Staff, G–2, Department of the Army; the Director of Naval Intelligence; and the Deputy Director for Intelligence, The Joint Staff, believe that:

   Although the performance characteristics are now unknown, they would very probably exceed those previously estimated (see NIE 11–6–54). It appears highly unlikely that the USSR would produce and employ missiles on the scale apparent from observation of the Moscow complexes without achieving, in their opinion, a substantial measure of defense against attacking aircraft.

   This belief is reinforced by evidence of the advanced state of Soviet developments in other missile fields, and the importance which the Soviets must attach to the development of a really effective air defense which would so greatly increase their strategic flexibility.

Allied tactical nuclear capabilities in Europe the USSR will probably give high priority to producing ballistic missiles for support of its field forces. However, aside from these missiles the USSR will probably concentrate over the next few years more on ballistic missile development than on quantity production. We estimate that: *(Paras. 18–20)*

a. *Short Range.* The USSR, in addition to shorter range ballistic missiles, could have had since 1954 an operational 350 mile ballistic missile with a CEP of two miles.[3] We believe that the USSR has not developed a 500 mile missile. *(Paras. 21–23)*

b. *Medium Range.* The USSR could have ready for series production in 1955–1956 a single-stage, ballistic missile of 850–900 miles range, with a CEP of three to four miles. However, only a low yield nuclear warhead probably would be available for the next few years. *(Paras. 24–25)*

c. *Intermediate Range Ballistic Missile (IRBM).* In 1958–1959 the USSR could have ready for series production a dual stage ballistic missile of about 1,600 miles range with a CEP of three to four miles. Large yield nuclear warheads would probably be available in 1959–1960. If the USSR were willing to accept a reduced range of 1,400 miles, this missile could be made ready for series production as early as 1957, but in this case only a low yield nuclear warhead would be available. *(Paras. 26–27)*

d. *Intercontinental Ballistic Missile (ICBM).* We now estimate that as soon as 1960–1961 the USSR could have ready for series production an intercontinental ballistic missile of 5,500 miles range, with a large yield nuclear warhead and a CEP of roughly five miles. Advent of such an ICBM would create an entirely new type of threat to the US. *(Para. 28)*

5. *Earth Satellite.* We estimate that the Soviets are attempting to develop such a vehicle at the earliest practicable date and could have a relatively uninstrumented vehicle by 1958. A vehicle which could gather and transmit upper atmosphere scientific data could be available by 1963. *(Paras. 29–30)*

6. *Air-to-Air Missiles.* We have no new intelligence which either strengthens or changes our estimate in NIE 11-6-54, that "because of its air defense weaknesses, the USSR is probably also assigning a very high priority to air-to-air missiles. We estimate that it could develop in 1955 a guided rocket with infrared homing and in 1955–1958 an improved version with greater range. However, their guidance system would permit only tail cone attacks under generally fair weather conditions at the engagement altitude. In 1958–1960 the USSR could probably have a new all-weather missile." *(Para. 31)*

7. *Air-to-Surface Missiles.* New intelligence partially supports estimates in NIE 11-6-54, but does not warrant a change therein. NIE 11-6-54 stated that "the USSR also would almost certainly seek to produce in quantity any precision weapon available for effective HE antiship attacks. For this purpose it could now have available and would probably produce a rocket-propelled glide bomb, although limited to good visibility condi-

---

[3] CEP (Circular Probable Error) means 50 percent hits within the stated radius. All CEPs and ranges are given in nautical miles.

tions. In view of its extensive bomber capabilities, we do not believe that the USSR would produce a long-range air-to-surface missile for attacks on Allied ports and bases over the next several years. In 1960, on the other hand, when we estimate that an all-weather air-to-surface missile with nuclear warhead could be ready for series production, there will probably be a high priority Soviet requirement for a weapon of this type because of the increased effectiveness of Allied air defenses around key target areas." *(Para. 32)*

8. *Submarine-Launched Missiles.* We have no credible new intelligence which either changes or strengthens our estimate in NIE 11-6-54 that "the USSR will almost certainly have a requirement for submarine-launched missiles for nuclear attacks on US and Allied coastal areas. It could already have available improved V-1 types with nuclear warheads. In 1955 the USSR could have ready for series production a turbo-jet pilotless aircraft (nonballistic guided missile) with improved range, speed, and accuracy, and by 1958 its nuclear warhead yield could approach compatibility with its estimated accuracy and greatly increase its effectiveness." *(Para. 33)*

DISCUSSION

9. In NIE 11-6-54 (dated 5 October 1954) we estimated that the strategic requirements of the USSR would dictate a major effort in the field of guided missiles, and that the USSR has the basic scientific and technical capabilities to support a comprehensive research and development program. We also estimated that the USSR has an adequate economic base for a sizeable production program; however, because of the limited capabilities of the Soviet electronics and precision mechanisms industries and other competing demands for their output it would almost certainly be unable to produce in the desired quantities all of the missiles for which it has an estimated military requirement, except over an extended period of years. Finally we estimated, on the basis of the large number of personalities and activities believed to be involved in the Soviet missile program and our knowledge of the extensive Soviet exploitation of German missile experience, that the Soviet program was an extensive one. However, we had no firm intelligence on what specific missiles the USSR was actually developing or might already have in operational use.

10. The intelligence which has become available subsequent to NIE 11-6-54 generally substantiates the above conclusions and reinforces our estimate that an extensive Soviet missile program is underway.[4] In the category of surface-to-surface ballistic missiles we now believe that Soviet progress has been somewhat more rapid than previously estimated and that such missiles, up to and including an ICBM, will become available at somewhat earlier dates. Moreover, new evidence indicates that the USSR has already embarked on series production of surface-to-air missiles.

I. SURFACE-TO-AIR MISSILES

11. The most significant development in this field is the extensive reporting on what appear to be air defense missile sites around Moscow. Allowing for probable duplication in reporting we estimate that approximately 40 complexes actually have been observed. The earliest observation of one of these sites was in mid-1953, with the majority being observed in late 1954 and 1955. Of these 40 sites, about 12 have been located with sufficient accuracy

---
Annex B (limited distribution) contains additional background information.